LapDog Therapy

My Journey from Companion Dog to Therapy Dog

by

Anchor's and RJ's Special Beau, C.G.C., T.D.I.

writing as

Mickey

Foreword by
H. Marie Suthers-McCabe, D.V.M.

Watercolors by
Paula R. Cameron, D.V.M.

Drawings by
Julie Parker

To
Winnie's and my friends at the Hermitage
and to
all other therapy dogs and their friends everywhere

Published with funds provided by
The Widgeon Foundation, Inc.

for

Center for Animal Human Relationships (CENTAUR)
Virginia-Maryland Regional College of Veterinary Medicine
Virginia Tech (Virginia Polytechnic Institute and State University)
Blacksburg, Virginia 24061

ISBN 0-9724880-0-6

Watercolors:
Paula R. Cameron, D.V.M. - pp. v, 1, 7, 11, 21, 33, 39, front cover

Drawings:
Julie Parker - pp. 10, 16, 18, 23, 24, 29, 31, 37
Dana Crandall, p. 27

Photo Credits:
Margaret Swan: pp. 4, 9, 36
Sarah Nock: pp. 30, 35

Photo Enhancement:
Evan Clements
Pam Gross, back cover

Other books by Mickey:
"A Boston's World" ISBN 1-879295-27-X

LapDog Therapy
(My Journey from Companion Dog to Therapy Dog)

CONTENTS

At www.vetmed.vt.edu/centaur, please download PowerPoint presentations appropriate for use with veterinarians and veterinary students; physicians, medical school students, nurses and nursing students; administrators of hospitals, retirement homes, and nursing homes; graduate and undergraduate students in healthcare administration; residents of healthcare facilities, retirement homes and healthcare communities; civic groups; therapy dogs and would be therapy dogs; therapy dog owners and would be therapy dogs owners; and dog lovers ad infinitum.

Most dogs practicing in hospitals today are certified either by Therapy Dogs International in New Jersey or by the Delta Society, a Seattle-based nonprofit organization that screens dogs for personality, obedience and training in hospital protocols. Delta estimates that its 4,500 "pet partners" have provided services for 350,000 patients in 45 states.

Margot Roosevelt
"Canine Candy Stripers"
Time Magazine, August 6, 2001

Introduction

A dog's love offers medicine for the spirit which may help heal the body.

Barrett Richardson
Unpublished manuscript

Therapy dogs serve as four-footed attitude adjustment specialists who make a real difference for those experiencing some of life's most difficult and trying times. These canine goodwill ambassadors are always happy to see their human charges, and it shows the minute they enter the room. Picked for their stable but friendly demeanor, therapy dogs' special gift is their willingness to interact with people.

Brian W. Swinn
"Paws for Healing"
Dog & Kennel, August 2001

FOREWORD
Forward! Heel! Foreword!
by

H. Marie Suthers-McCabe, D.V.M.
Associate Professor, Human-Companion Animal Interaction
Director, Center for Animal Human Relationships (CENTAUR)
Virginia-Maryland Regional College of Veterinary Medicine
Virginia Tech (Virginia Polytechnic Institute and State University)

Who should read this book?

• **Dog lovers** and **people lovers** alike will enjoy this new perspective on animal-assisted activities - straight from a therapy dog's mouth and mind.
• **Professionals in healthcare administration** will benefit from the well thought out detail in this comprehensive in-depth review of the life of a therapy dog.
• **Educators of both human health and veterinary health care teams** will be able to generate student discourse about animal-assisted activities and therapy with the encouragement of the PowerPoint presentations written for this book.
• **Therapists, counselors, physicians and veterinarians** will find a fresh approach to an aspect of their chosen professions.
• **Residents of long-term care facilities** will find joy in the many anecdotes and in the delightful watercolors by veterinarian Paula Cameron.
• Even the **family dog** may benefit from this book. The dog in your lap may be a potential therapy dog. This book can help these dogs reach their full potential by educating their owners. Read this book to your dog and work through the steps necessary to determine if he or she would be appropriate for and enjoy this work.

Meet Mickey, a Boston Terrier who favors cream cheese treats, enjoys sniffing daffodils, and loves to write words as much as fetch balls. After a brief show dog career as *Anchor's and RJ's Special Beau*, Mickey went to live in a non-show home. Here he discovered the computer in the loft and his penchant for writing. "It's like playing ball," Mickey writes, "I play with an idea the way I play with a ball. To find the best words for an idea, I look at the possibilities dancing around in the air, snatch the best ones out of the blue, toss them around, jump at them sideways, take pretend bites, and finally grab whatever I want, running with it as fast as I can." When Mickey heard about animal-assisted therapy he knew right away this was an idea he wanted to run with. He soon discovered that it was multifaceted and that he had a lot to learn to reach his goal.

foreward continued

Allow Mickey to place the end of his leash in your hand and to lead you through his personal transformation from a mere but wonderful companion dog to a lap-top therapy dog. By following Mickey and his partner Winnie, you will be introduced to the growing world of animal-assisted activities and therapy. This is a world of compassion, friendship and smiles.

You will discover the many benefits derived from providing animal-assisted activities. A major benefit is *socialization*. The dog helps "break the ice" as the volunteer introduces him or her to a resident. The dog becomes the *focus* of attention helping everyone get acquainted. Residents focus on the dog and the volunteer. While doing this, they tend to forget about their problems. Dogs bring out *compassion* in those who may not be as compassionate toward human beings. Many times there is an instant *friendship* established between the resident and dog. This friendship carries over to the volunteer who is visiting with his dog. Petting the dog feels safe, warm and non-threatening to residents. Seeing and petting a dog may bring out a *nurturing* or parenting instinct in those visited. Visiting with a dog is *mentally stimulating* to the resident. Communication increases when a resident meets the therapy dog. Dogs *accept* others unconditionally, disregarding an individual's looks, mobility, and medical conditions. Dogs are *entertaining*. Just their presence in an assisted living or nursing home facility brings smiles to residents' faces. Dogs used in animal-assisted therapy bring additional benefits to residents. Therapists address specific treatment goals. Some physical goals may be to use dogs to help improve a resident's strength and endurance, range of motion of joints, sensations, or balance and mobility. Also, cognitive and perceptual deficiencies may be addressed.

Allow yourself to be led through the mechanics, joys and rewards of animal assisted activities with a therapy dog named Mickey and his partner Winnie and prepare to embark on a new life-enriching adventure. Woof.

Preface
How Mickey and Winnie Became Involved in Lapdog Therapy
by
Anne Nock

By nature, a dog has an uncanny ability to tune in to the needs of a human being. In fact, dogs can be counted on to supply therapy intuitively in the form of a listening ear, a loving lick, an understanding heart and a warm body for cuddling. A person doesn't have to be physically sick, emotionally disturbed, or clinically depressed for a dog's soulful eyes to awaken within him an instantaneous connection with life itself that draws him out of himself and back into the world.

When illness or age forces people to slow down, it seems that being able to connect with something living means more than anything else. The living thing can be a dandelion, a rose, a dog, a cat, or a human, but a dog seems to tug at a person's heart-strings in a particularly winsome way that no other animal, person, or living thing can match. This may explain why something almost magical happens when Winnie and Mickey make therapy rounds. Without fail, the faces of residents and employees alike break into smiles as soon as they see the dogs. The most withdrawn person will look their way and smile

If dogs enjoy being with people, if they are reasonably calm and generally obedient, they are good candidates for therapy dog training and work. If they love children, their therapy work might center in a children's hospital or a home for physically handicapped children or mentally disturbed children. If they are comfortable around older people, their therapy efforts might be focused in a retirement or nursing home, assisted living facility, or senior day care center. Time and time again, if used on an

Mickey greeted Mrs. Betty Dean and her husband on the day they moved into their new apartment.

The bond between dogs and people has been forged by 15,000 years of mutual admiration and mutual trust. Civilizations have risen and fallen, the terrifying unknown has been explored, the great obstacles to human progress surmounted. And it has all been done with the dog – partner, companion, protector – at our side. Dogs don't steal our hearts: we surrendered our hearts to them long, long ago.

Tom Davis
Why Dogs Do That
Willow Creek Press, 1998

preface continued

A good feeling comes over Mrs. Bernice Gouget when she touches Winnie's little foot.

ongoing basis, therapy dogs have proved they can make a big difference in the lives of people of any age. My two Boston Terriers, Winnie and Mickey, are therapy dogs working with elderly people in a nearby continuing care retirement community. Because several of my friends living there often referred to family dogs they had loved in their earlier lives when I stopped in to see them, I began to take Winnie and Mickey with me on my visits. Although I did not fully realize at first how meaningful those visits were to residents, I soon came to see that Winnie and Mickey could often provide my friends with a stimulus for conversation, a distraction from pain, and a diversion from monotony that I was unable to offer. When other residents invited us to visit with them, we jumped at the chance.

Mickey has written <u>LapDog Therapy</u> to suggest to both professionals and lay people that greater efforts could be made to bring therapy dogs into the lives of institutionalized and homebound people. Mickey hopes that his book will be a catalyst in making it possible for more elderly people living in retirement homes, continuing care communities, nursing homes and hospitals to enjoy the company of a dog or to pet and be comforted by a dog's warm body. If the humans in medical, veterinary and counselor-therapy circles were to join hands and hearts with dogs and their owners in addressing the needs of people whose mobility is severely restricted or who are becoming withdrawn from social interaction, these people would benefit immeasurably from the love dogs offer.

It is at this point that my Preface ends and Mickey begins to write.

As proven by Chase, Cody, Winston, Tootsie and Jillian – and by countless dogs worldwide – therapy can walk in on four paws with a dog's soft breath, a lick, a snuggle and a gentle touch. Although we all love the simple warmth and happiness that the bond between dogs and humans brings us, it does even more: it is, truly, a healing bond.

Darlene Arden
"The Healing Bond"
AKC Gazette, October 2000

CHAPTER I
Getting Started

Forget laughter. Animals are the best medicine.

Roberta Taylor, LPN
Sussex County LPN Program Pharmacology Worksheet

Dogs – who possess their own form of communication through barks, tail wags and body language – are also well skilled in the art of active listening. They are only too pleased to respond to human touch or gesture with an ear twitch or a tail wag.

Communication with a dog also offers "safe" touch. In days when hospital policies and procedures are concerned with the issue of human relationship boundaries, canine touch is not only acceptable but pleasurable. The touch of a dog provides, quite literally, those warm fuzzy feelings that patients with aphasia need.

Canines can also assist in the philosophy of rehabilitation. . . .

A review of the literature attests to the power of dogs to facilitate communication. It has been found, for instance, that people walking with a dog experience more social contact and longer conversations than when walking alone. Wheelchair-users – some of whom are aphasic – are more likely to experience positive social interactions with a dog.

Julianne Labreche
Best Friends, Therapy Dogs Helping Aphasic Adults
Primrose Court Publications, 2001

I Learn to be a Canine Good Citizen (CGC)

I can remember that first night of school as clearly as if it was yesterday. There we were, all twelve of us dogs, assembled with our owners in the fenced-in athletic field of a nearby high school. We were yapping and straining on our leashes, pulling this way and that. How would I ever learn anything in the midst of such a riot? I've always had a deep trust in my mom – ever since I became her dog when I was ten months old – but I was really wondering at this point about her judgment in having signed us up for "Canine Good Citizen" school. CGC is a standardized course sponsored nationwide by the American Kennel Club (AKC). If this was what school was all about, I knew I didn't like it!

The SPCA where I live sponsors a CGC course every spring in which young dogs learn good citizenship manners. That first night, it was evident all of us needed the class, but I hadn't imagined such chaos. To boot, I was sort of scared. Suppose one of the big dogs tried to take a bite out of me? I'd never been so close to so many different kinds of dogs - big and little; short-coated, curly-coated and long-coated; pointy noses and flat ones; splotchy spots and solid colors.

As soon as our teacher, Mrs. Linda Pruitt, spoke, however, I loved the sound of her voice and began to wonder if I might have a good time after all. Before I knew it, Mrs. Pruitt had showed us how to sit quietly at the left side of our owners. Why the left side instead of the right? Maybe because most people are right-handed. Anyhow, it didn't make any difference to me on which side we "heeled" and on which side we sat when we heard the word "halt." I just tried to follow directions whatever they were and not run into the next dog!

Soon most of us got the idea, though there were a few who continued to balk at Mrs. Pruitt's directions. We were supposed to walk along close on the left side of our owners. If they turned or stopped suddenly, we were supposed to turn or stop also. It was like a game for me to guess from the way my mom moved whether she was about to speed up, slow down or stop. When I pretended we were hooked together by a little strip of velcro, staying in step was fun.

Each week during the course, Mrs. Pruitt introduced a new CGC requirement by demonstrating with Lady, her Golden Retriever, what we were supposed to learn. Lady could almost read Mrs. Pruitt's mind. She did everything Mrs. Pruitt asked of her exactly right. By the time our eight weeks of classes were over, we had settled down and learned to greet friendly strangers without jumping on them; to heel on a leash in the presence of other dogs and people, even in a crowd; to sit and lie down on command and stay in those positions until we heard an "Okay, Good Dog;" to come when called and sit facing our owners right square in front of them – then to swing around to the heeling position on command. We also learned what "NO BARK" meant. That alone cut the confusion down considerably.

You might think it would be easy to learn how to heel, sit/stay and down/stay (even if you want to get up and go somewhere else), come when called, and so on. But it takes a lot of concentration and determination on the part of a dog and owner to master these concepts. Believe me when I say we practiced at home every day between classes because I wanted to get it right.

Mrs. Pruitt and Lady are
wonderful teachers

Winnie's CGC School Experience

Winnie is more laid back than I am

Winnie had a whole different attitude about school. She had had a puppy socialization class–like kindergarten for kids—that should have helped prepare her for CGC school. But Winnie did not like school from the first day, and she never changed her mind. She found it hard to concentrate and often did not appear to comprehend whatever task or exercise she was supposed to be learning. Winnie's not dumb–I think she just didn't apply herself. Her progress was exceedingly slow for whatever reason—her lack of interest, refusal to pay attention or ineptness. However, when she retook the course a year later, Winnie passed the CGC test, and she also qualified as a therapy dog under the guidelines of TDI, Therapy Dogs International.

Because Winnie seemed to be a slow learner in school, I had misgivings whether she would ever be an effective therapy dog. Surprise of all surprises, Winnie loves therapy work and is good at it! This goes to show, I think, that you can't always tell how a dog's life will turn out from his performance in school.

Looking back, I see now how important the CGC course was. First, it taught us how to act in any situation which has stood us in good stead whatever the circumstances. Secondly, it put us on track for therapy dog training and membership.

It is likely there is a CGC course available close to almost every dog in the country because the AKC promotes it nationwide. To determine where CGC classes are being taught in your area, visit the AKC website, www.akc.org. If you'd like to know more about the CGC course, see the book, <u>Canine Good Citizen</u> by Jack and Wendy Volhard, ISBN 0-87605-420-3, which explains in great detail every step of the process of becoming a CGC dog.

There are ten parts to the CGC test:

<u>*Canine Good Citizens Test*</u>
1. Accept a friendly stranger
2. Sit politely for petting
3. Be well groomed
4. Walk (heel) on a loose leash
5. Walk through a crowd
6. Sit on command/stay in place
7. Come when called
8. React to another dog calmly
9. Remain calm when startled by unexpected noises & actions
10. Remain calm during supervised separation from owner.

adapted from Your Dog, A Magazine for Caring Dog Owners, Tufts University School of Veterinary Medicine, September 2000, Vol. VI, No. 9.

The American Kennel Club's Canine Good Citizen program was developed to promote responsible dog ownership in a manner that would be easy for both dog and owner....By providing certification to both pure-bred dogs and mixed breeds, the CGC encompasses all dogs affected by canine legislation.

Jack and Wendy Volhard
The Canine Good Citizen
Howell Book House, 1994

Winnie's kindergarten class

Therapy Dogs International, Inc. (TDI)

Toward the end of the CGC course, my teacher began to bring wheelchairs and walkers to class, and she asked some of her friends to visit us and use the wheelchairs and walkers during our schooling. Our part was to keep our minds on our lessons in the midst of the pretend nursing home scenario created by her friends. To become a real Therapy Dog, added to the successful completion of the CGC course, we had to prepare for a therapy dog test. You can't just appear at the door of a hospital or retirement home and say you want to practice therapy. You'd never get in.

Dogs of all shapes and sizes can be therapy dogs.

We chose Therapy Dogs International (TDI) because TDI is the therapy organization for which Mrs. Pruitt is an authorized evaluator. The paws-on test was designed to prove we had learned how a dog should act around senior citizens. After many hours of practice, both of us passed. We realized later, however, that taking the test was easy: the hard part was remembering everything we'd learned in school, especially the rule about not being distracted when we are on the job.

As TDI dogs, we received official photo ID cards, TDI insurance coverage and bright yellow TDI collar tags. We feel very important with the tags bobbing against our chests.

TDI was organized in 1976 to make dogs' love and companionship available to hospital/nursing home patients and retirement home residents. With headquarters in Flanders, New Jersey, TDI has people members, dog members and certified evaluators all over the world. To provide continuing education resources for its members as well as information about their therapeutic activities, TDI issues a newsletter three times per year. TDI isn't the only Animal Therapy organization, though, and each has its own requirements for membership. Some of the others are Therapy Dogs, Inc., Foundation for Pet Provided Therapy, Paws for Health, the Delta Society Pet Partners, Alpha Affiliates, Inc. and Pets on Wheels. (See information for organizations on pp. 41-46)

People are attracted to the sight of a dog. Filmmakers use this device frequently—sometimes having a dog move across the screen for no other reason than to get you to look! If you walk with your dog, you have surely noticed how people are drawn to it. This helps illustrate how a therapy dog can have the power to bring disoriented people into the moment. Some Alzheimer's sufferers and other people whose minds wander benefit from being brought mentally into the here and now as often as possible....The dog can give them both a focal point and a reason to try (to focus).

Kathy Diamond Davis
Therapy Dog
Howell, 1992

Our Therapy Dog Practice

Two years went by before Winnie and I had a chance to do some paws-on therapy dog practice – not in a continuing care retirement community but in our own home at first and then at our grandmother's house. When the debilitating effects of cancer slowed our dad's activities to a standstill, Winnie and I sprang into action. Realizing Dad seemed to hurt less when he was loving us, we stayed with him more, either in his lap or in a chair pulled up close beside him.

We expanded our therapy dog role with our grandmother by giving her lots of slurpy kisses when we visited. At that time we also discovered how much fun it is to walk beside a wheelchair. Before that, we had gone bananas around wheels of any kind, especially bicycle wheels. But escorting a wheelchair with Dad or our grandmother was different. We loved it. In addition to being sick physically, our grandmother was sometimes confused. The fact that she was mixed up about some things didn't bother us at all because she was always glad to see us. She'd smile when we walked up to her and always invited us to jump up in her lap.

Later, Winnie and I wondered if we might be able to comfort elderly people living in a continuing care retirement community where they can't have dogs living with them. We knew there was such a place not far from our house. We thought about how we could get in to try out our home therapy on a bigger scale. So, the next time Mom tried to leave us in the car when she visited there, we yapped so much that she took us out for a walk. It worked. We walked over to the entrance and right through the door! Sometimes you have to speak up to be heard. That's how we got in to start practicing therapy in a group living environment. Our early weekly visits turned out to be sort of a "therapy dog residency" when we got first-paw experience visiting with lots of different people.

The more we have worked as therapy dogs, the more we've come to understand the residents' needs and what we can do for them. We're helping them see that some of the changes in life they fear the most, such as—that the world doesn't come to an end when they move out of their own homes—aren't nearly as bad as they thought.

Of the many services dogs provide to humans, possibly the most important service–and the one they do best–is to lift the human spirit.

Carolyn Alexander
"My Mother's Gift" Dog Heroes
AKC Gazette, October 2000

**Winnie used to ride in our grandmother's lap.
I always liked to walk beside her wheelchair
where I could keep watch.**

Chapter II
Terminology

Just as environmentalists consider the South American rain forest to be the lungs of the Earth, providing all living creatures with the oxygen necessary for respiration, I believe that, as we learn more about our connection to animals, we will consider them our heart. More than anything else on this earth, animals have the facility to make sure we remain connected to our deepest feelings.

Allen M. Schoen, D.V.M., M.S.
Kindred Spirits

An amiable, docile dog, the highly intelligent Boston Terrier is easily trained, full of character, and a good guard dog.

A boisterous dog, it is full of fun with a liking for playing with toys.

David Taylor, editor
The Family Dog.
Barron's, 2001

The Boston Terrier is very special to me because my diabetic son's Boston, Elsa, may have saved his life one night before he got an insulin pump to dispense insulin around the clock. Sensing that something was terribly wrong with my son one night as he slept, Elsa barked and barked to arouse him and his wife as my son's blood sugar dropped dangerously low. At a time when James couldn't help himself, Elsa helped him. I'll always look on the Boston breed as sensitive, caring and intelligent.

Uta Wilbur
Interview, 2001

Do You Know the Difference between a Therapy Dog and a Service Dog?

There is a clear distinction between the terms *therapy dog* and *service dog* which many people do not understand, although most dogs do. Let me explain it in terms of human school: therapy dogs have the equivalent of high school diplomas; service dogs have college degrees and even graduate degrees. Although the dividing line between the two degrees is sometimes fuzzy, service dogs are trained usually to provide specific services for their owners, whereas therapy dogs work with their owners to offer good will to *other* people.

It is much easier to become a therapy dog than a service dog.

A therapy dog must pass the AKC Canine Good Citizen Course or simiar certification and a therapy dog test, but that's the end of his school work. Additionally, our personalities must be generally suited for therapy work (whether with adults or children) with calm temperament, good manners, and pleasant disposition, but we are not taught a specific way of performing a particular service. It is possible that an unusually sharp therapy dog might learn, on his own, to alert his owner to an alarming situation or condition, and that could be likened to a service. But the work of most therapy dogs is directed to *other* people by a team composed of the dog and his co-worker owner. Or to put it another way, a therapy dog is sort of like a cruise ship recreation director who encourages passengers to participate in available activities.

A service dog, on the other paw, is trained to perform a specific service for a specific person who is usually his constant companion and owner. In addition to having the right disposition for the job, the dog must be able to catch on quickly to whatever tasks he needs to learn. For example, a guide dog is taught to safely guide a visually impaired person around obstacles as he walks, and a service dog for the hearing impaired learns to alert his owner to a telephone ring or a doorbell chime. Other service dogs work with wheelchair-bound people, fetching articles or performing various tasks.

In a more dramatic way, dogs assume heroic search-and-rescue roles during war, earthquakes and criminal assaults, or provide back-up to human partners during drug raids and sniffing out bombs. War duty especially requires both stamina and bravery of rescue dogs. As witnessed after the 9/11 World Trade Towers/Pentagon attack, search-and-rescue dogs played a gigantic role in the recovery operation, and therapy dogs, too, were on the scene to help. I sometimes wonder what it would be like to be a service dog. However, I'm not a spring chicken anymore. I think I'll stick with my first career – therapy dog.

Dogs have the ability to radiate compassion and sympathy in times of great human need. Dogs certified as therapy dogs are qualified to make visits to hospitals, rehabilitation facilities, nursing homes, schools and prisons. Now they appear to include disaster sites to their roster, adding their expertise to the legions of mental health workers, ministers and other counselors, aiding the grief-stricken families and rescuers.

Leslie Crane Rugg
Canine Nature, The Spirit That Keeps Giving
Dog & Kennel, April 2002

The Acronyms, AFT, AAT, AAA, and PAT

Whether you are looking up therapy dog organizations on the Internet or reading about them in a magazine or book, you'll want to understand some basic terms. If you want to dig further, check out a therapy dog book from your public library (see Bibliography, p. 47). Perhaps the most detailed book I have ever seen on the subject of therapy dogs is Aubrey Fine's Handbook on Animal-Assisted Therapy. In addition to covering lots of history, it gives results of case studies and clinical tests in which therapy dogs were used. I am especially glad it spells out what the therapy acronyms stand for, because they are confusing.

-*AFT* (animal-facilitated therapy) covers the entire range of animal-supplied therapy that takes place in retirement homes, hospitals, rehabilitation centers and private homes. AFT is considered old terminology in the field of human-animal interaction.

-*AAT* (animal assisted therapy) is offered by a volunteer and his dog who assist health professionals – or a professional therapist with his own trained dog – working in a prescribed program that addresses the specific needs of a particular person whose world has been whittled away due to illness and/or age. Careful written records are kept of all AAT sessions which are an integral part of the person's overall treatment plan, and these records become part of the patient's case history.

-*AAA* (animal assisted activities) and *PAT* (pet assisted therapy) refer to therapy provided by layman volunteers who take their own dogs (and sometimes cats) to bring cheer to people who are elderly and/or sick or to sick children. *AAA* and *PAT* are not directed by professionals nor are written records necessarily kept of each visit. *AAA* refers to the use of any animal whether dog, cat, rabbit or guinea pig in therapy work, and *PAT* refers specifically to *Pet* Animal Therapy. AAA is considered old terminology in the field of human-animal interaction.

...volunteers find it rewarding to share their animals with others who enjoy them to the point that many make commitments to visit facilities on a routine weekly basis. It is important to note that such remarkable motivation probably would not occur if the person were visiting the nursing home alone. The animal partner is the essential participant that makes the effort of the volunteer worthwhile.

Lynette A. Hart
Chapter 4, "Psychosocial Benefits of Animal-Assisted Therapy"
Handbook of Animal-Assisted Therapy by Aubrey Fine, Academic Press, 2000

CHAPTER III
Therapy Visits in a Healthcare Facility in a Resident's Room or Apartment

Life in a nursing home can be lonely. Some studies estimate that well over half of nursing home residents never receive visitors. Some caring dog owners and their pets are working to put an end to the loneliness of nursing home residents, as well as hospitalized children, patients in pyschiatric wards, and anyone else who is in some way institutionalized and could use a friendly, furry head to pat.

Joel Walton and Eve Adamson
Labrador Retrievers for Dummies

Therapy dogs go with their owners to visit patients at hospitals or nursing homes, generally remaining on leash but able to coax a pat from a stiffened hand, a smile from a blank face, a few words from sealed lips or a hug from someone in need of love.

Scottee Meade
The Boston Terrier
Howell Book House, 2000

Some People Don't Like Dogs

We've always known there are people who don't care much for dogs. It doesn't matter what the dogs look like, how large or small they are, if they are clean or dirty, or how cunning they are – some people simply have no use for dogs under any circumstances. So be it. I feel the same way about some people. Before making our first visit to the retirement home, we worried a little whether residents and staff would like us hanging around.

Some residents ignored us from the very beginning. They didn't have to say, "Don't come near me, I don't like dogs" for us to get the picture. If they held up a shaky stop-sign hand or shuddered, or just looked the other way when we approached them, we knew they weren't interested in being friends. As it turned out, we shouldn't have been apprehensive because many more people welcomed us than not.

To get our bearings on that first visit, Mrs. Helenann Moore, Resident Services Director, had prepared a list of residents who were animal lovers. Mrs. Moore's information kept us from hitting too many road blocks in the beginning which would have been discouraging. And now, as new residents come in, Mrs. Moore continues to advise us as to their feelings about dogs.

Also, Mrs. Moore had explained to the staff about our impending visit. Because the Eden Alternative had been introduced some years before with the establishment of Petie-bird's residence (see p. 26 and www.edenalt.com for more about the Eden Alternative), many of the staff already knew the basics of animal-assisted therapy and were supportive of our visits from the first day.

**When we are not invited to come in,
we look for a more friendly doorway.**

The relationships between people and animals are complex, multi-determinate, and changing. The use of animals to help people with special needs is an example of physiological and psychological symbiosis at work, part of a millennia-old evolution. At first, we saw animals as gods, then as slaves, then as workers: today many of us see them as companions, our partners on this planet we call Earth.

**Phil Arkow
Pet Therapy
Arkow, 8th Edition, 1998**

Checking In

Hi!

It's always a good idea to check in at the front desk. At our retirement home, we go straight to Muriel Scott, the receptionist, who gives us an up-to-date schedule of the day's activities. Although we try to visit when other activities aren't planned, last-minute changes can happen anytime that play havoc with the regular schedule. A dog must be flexible and go with the flow.

Because it usually takes senior citizens a long time to get ready for an event, we don't ever try to squeeze in a quick visit just before another event is scheduled. Although this cuts down on available time for our visits, it works best for everybody. The good we could do by spending time with friends would be compromised if they felt pushed or hurried during our visit. In therapy work, "relaxation" is a very important word.

The receptionist keeps track of changes in the daily schedule.

If you end up being one of the 4 percent of the elderly population in a rest home, your family should look for one that allows you to bring your animals with you, has them visit regularly, or has a few residing there.

Marty Becker, D.V.M
The Healing Power of Pets
Hyperion, 2002

A Love Lick
Introduce yourself gently

Many people think therapy dogs have to be large dogs. That's probably because guide dogs for the visually impaired usually are large, so people often think of big breeds like German Shepherds and Collies when they hear the term "therapy dog" or "service dog." Actually, guide dogs are service animals trained to perform a specific function for a specific person, whereas therapy dogs offer general good will to many people.

While it is true that big dogs can be very effective therapy dogs, I think we small breeds have some advantages over them. One is that people not used to dogs aren't automatically afraid when they first see us because we don't look threatening. Another is that one of us, or even both of us, can fit in a person's lap. A Rottweiler, much less a pair of Rottweilers, could never do that and shouldn't even try.

When Winnie and I come upon persons whom we have never visited before, we stand quietly or sit very still in front of them for a minute or two. Because I'm so full of energy, I seem sort of jumpy sometimes when I move. Because Winnie is more graceful than I am, she is usually the one to make the first move which will be offering a love lick or two. Chances are good that a love lick will be enough to break the ice. We'll gain a new friend who will start to notice us and even call us by name the next time we pass by. We've learned that most people will talk to us if we give them time even if they don't seem interested at first. If a person ignores us completely, we visit again on another day.

Winnie introduces herself gently to
Mrs. Marybelle Badger.

Gus needed a living link to the dog he'd once loved; Rowdy was his animate time machine. Nancy's need was raw and primitive. She suffered from the depletion of life itself. Rowdy was her donor, like a blood donor, really, but a transfuser of vitality that you could almost see and touch as it shot from him to her and restored, however briefly, her powers of speech and reason.

Susan Conant
The Barker Street Regulars
Bantam Books, 1999

Watching Television
Pick up an activity in progress

A therapy dog doesn't actually have to do anything to be helpful. We've heard there are medical and psychological benefits for people who simply have dogs available for loving. The unconditional love we offer makes people feel good about themselves even when they are hurting. Because we often can do the job that medicine would do, they don't have to swallow any pills.

When we make a therapy visit, we try to fit ourselves into whatever the person is doing. For example, a television program can set the stage for us. If a person is glued to a television set, we watch tv. Sometimes I feel like Sherlock Holmes as I try to read a person's mind. However, if the television is on, any therapy dog would know simply to hop up in the person's lap (a large breed would sidle up as close as possible beside the person) and watch the show, too! Winnie loves to watch TV, especially when she is in somebody's lap.

Before Mrs. Frances Kjerner moved to our retirement home, her little terrier, Peter Pumpkin, watched television with her in her other home. Mrs. Kjerner feels happier with a dog in her lap than when she watches television alone. Mainly, we just sit quietly as the person pats us or rubs our coats, but when a kiss is asked for, we oblige.

**Mrs. Kjerner and Winnie like
some of the same tv shows**

Pets, dogs especially, are tuned in to all those modes of communication that humans sometimes neglect. Compared to us, these animals keep things simple – a happy tone, a playful stance, a touch of the nose, and enough said. Pets have no room for...pity, scorn, judgment, and standards of beauty – all things we fear from our fellow humans. And it is when we are at our most vulnerable – old, sick, alone, in pain – that freedom from our fears can provide the most benefit. For some, animals give a rare sense of unconditional love. Exchanging affection with animals encourages people to be who they are and experience something wholly positive. And that makes people happy. And that makes people healthy.

**Catharine Mayor Lamm
Introduction
You Have a Visitor
Renee Lamm Esordi
Blue Lamm Publishing, 2000**

Always Accommodating
Stimulate memory with role play

A therapy dog tries to be receptive to reasonable requests made by residents. Therefore, we like to get to know a person in order to learn what he or she wants from us. We try to be accommodating, but I draw the line when it comes to pretending I am a baby. If that's what a person enjoys, I take a side seat while Winnie comes to the fore. She thinks playing baby is wonderful.

Role playing such as this helps bring to mind happy times of a person's earlier life. When we help trigger the recall of memories, the person often seems to be more connected to the present as he thinks about his or her memories and talks about them.

When we go to Mrs. Josephine Justis's room, Winnie loves to pretend she is Mrs. Justis's sweet little baby. The two of them always have a lot to talk about, and this frees me to concentrate on the squirrels that are up in the trees outside her window. From her room, I can see squirrels jumping and running in every direction. Something gets into me when I see a squirrel, and to see five or ten squirrels at one time tests any dog. But I remember my therapy dog training, sit quietly instead of flying through the window, and try not to disrupt Mrs. Justis's conversation with Winnie.

Watching, stroking, playing with, or talking to your pet has an immediately beneficial effect on your body. Just being with a pet reduces blood pressure and lowers anxiety.

Janet Ruckert
The Four-Footed Therapist
Ten Speed Press, 1987

It's true. Absolute. Fundamental.
A dog who's perceptive and gentle
(When there is no pill—
To knock out an ill)—
Can offer up love complimental!

A Special Friend of Bostons
Trigger conversation

Every dog, whether purebred or mutt, is attractive and loving in one way or another. Winnie and I respect all dogs regardless of their looks or breeding. It's not important how you look but how you act! Any dog, from Chihuahua to Great Dane, can become a therapy dog by passing the required tests. Once a dog gets the hang of figuring out the puzzle – what to do that will make each person smile and relax – he's got it made! We don't always have a 100% success story but usually we can help a person lighten up a little if not a whole lot.

When Winnie and I enter a resident's room, we like to walk side by side. We march straight over to the resident's chair or bed and stop. As soon as the person starts talking to us, we move in closer. One of us will jump up in his lap if we are invited to do so – or we sit attentively on the floor if that seems to be a good idea.

In theory, a therapy dog should treat all clients alike. We try to do that, but we feel a closer bond with some people than others. Mrs. Helen Taylor understands us unusually well because both of her grand-dogs, Buddy and Dolly, are dogs like us. When we visit Mrs. Taylor, she sometimes tells us about Dolly's and Buddy's latest antics. We always like to bring her up to date about what's going on in our lives – such as our medical checkups last week, for example, and sometimes we share with her some of our secret thoughts about life.

Mrs. Taylor's two grand-dogs look just like us!

Pets provide unconditional and non-judgmental love and affection to the human recipient. In the human society, a person's worth is too often judged by superficial characteristics: the ideal of beauty, youth, perceived status, or possessions. For those who do not fit the ideal mold, love can be automatically withheld.

The love an animal gives...is dictated by no such notions. A dog...will accept a tender stroke from an aged trembling hand as enthusiastically as from that of a young and able athlete. Also, a dog puts no conditions on its affection. Love is not withheld or denied if the owner does not perform in a satisfactory manner. The love that an animal gives comes free of strings and conditions; it is open, honest, straightforward, uncomplicated, and not subject to change.

Odean Cusack and Elaine Smith
Pets and the Elderly
Haworth Press, 1984

Even When a Person Still Owns a Dog
Focus on the present and the past

Mrs. Mary Whippo may be the luckiest person at our retirement home because she still owns a dog, Cassie, although she and Cassie no longer live in the same place. When Mrs. Whippo moved to the retirement home, Cassie, her scruffy, black, mixed-breed, moved nearby to Mrs. Whippo's daughter's and son-in-law's home. Their Golden Retriever, Jordan, and Cassie come to visit Mrs. Whippo whenever they can get a ride.

Sometimes when we first enter Mrs. Whippo's room, she seems to be daydreaming. But as soon as she sees us, she begins to tell us stories about some of the fun things Cassie and Jordan like to do. She laughs out loud when she thinks about the first time she saw baby Cassie at age ten weeks, and she loves to talk about Cassie's special tricks – how she sits up to beg for a treat and how she can toss a puppy bone treat up in the air and catch it. Winnie and I listen closely to her stories because they are so interesting. We can tell she feels better when she is telling us about Cassie because of the way her face glows. We always include Mrs. Whippo when we make our rounds because she loves to see us.

Mrs. Whippo talks with Cassie (l) and Jordan (r)

A dog is like a living photo album, bringing back memories of special dogs and good times in the past.

Kim Thornton and Virginia Guidry
For the Love of Dogs
Publications International, Ltd., 1997

Our Therapist
Therapy is a two-way street

Mrs. Lane is truly special to Winnie and me. Before we even poke our noses in her door, she calls out to us, "Hi Winnie! Hi Mickey! Come in." It always surprises me that she knows we are walking down the hall before we get to her apartment. Maybe she hears the little ruffling snorts I make when I'm excited. Anyhow, she seems to be able to hear better than anybody else we know!

We never have to nuzzle Mrs. Lane's shoe to get her attention.   Mrs. Lane usually starts talking to us as we approach her, and when we enter her room, she stops whatever she's doing to give us her full attention. It doesn't matter how busy Mrs. Lane is — whether she is knitting, listening to music, reading a talking book, or doing fancy handwork–when we arrive, she tunes us in. Sometimes, people keep on doing whatever they happen to be involved with and just notice us a little on the side, but not Mrs. Lane. Because she is so interested in us, we often feel that she is our therapist instead of the other way around.

Her touch is different, too. Other people pat us on the head with their fingers pushed together as if they were in a mitten. Not so with Mrs. Lane. She seems to feel our coats with the tips of her fingers. Mom says it is because she sees us with her fingers, not her eyes!

The elderly seem particularly to benefit from dogs who give their lives purpose, meaning, and a felt sense of love and connection.

Bonnie Bergin
Understanding "Dog Mind"
Little, Brown and Company, 2000

Mrs. Lane seems to have special feeling in her fingers.

CHAPTER IV

Therapy Visits in a Healthcare Facility outside a Resident's Room or Apartment

A wonderful thing about dogs is their ability to help other people, particularly those who need the kind of unconditional love that only a dog can give. I've seen faces of children in hospitals and elderly in nursing homes transformed from hopeless to radiant by one visit from a small, wet-nosed pet-assisted therapy dog.

Bash Dibra
Dog Speak
Simon & Schuster, 1999

It's well known in the medical community that animal visits to long-term care facilities (nursing homes, mental illness facilities, etc.) often bring about tremendous reactions from the patients. Therapy dogs can usually get patients who are socially closed off to interact and help them to create personal relationships.

Carlo DeVito and Amy Ammen
The Everything Dog Book
Copyright © 1998 Adams Media Corporation
Used by Permission of Adams Media Corporation

In the Beauty Parlor/Barber Shop
Grooming is important

Therapy dogs visit residents, not only in their rooms, but also in the lobby, halls, workshop, craft room, or library as well as outside. One of Winnie's favorite places to come upon a friend is in the beauty parlor/barber shop because she is always wishing for a new hairdo. She thinks she'll be in line for a makeover if she jumps up in the chair with Mr. Frank Cisar. I can tell Winnie's mind is on her own hair style – not on how she might help Mr. Cisar! When she gets distracted like this, I try to cover for her until she remembers her therapy dog training.

Because we should be clean when we make therapy rounds, we take baths the night before unless we are already sparkling clean. Nothing would make Winnie happier than to jump in the bathtub every day. That's a girl for you. But as much as I dislike baths, I understand the reason we must be bathed and groomed before setting paw in our retirement home. And our toenails have to be clipped and smoothed, too, lest we scratch somebody.

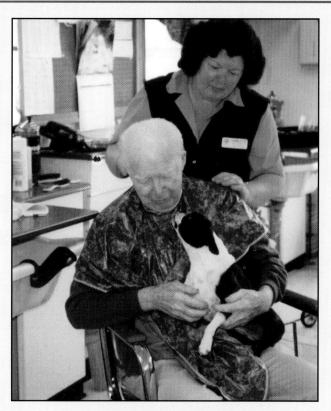

Winnie does therapy anywhere, especially if she thinks she might get a new hairdo out of it.

Animals make us feel loved and less alone.

In the Library
Read together

Part of our job description in animal assisted activities is to stimulate residents' thinking by helping them relax and talk to us. Just as a book can open new worlds for a reader, a dog all by himself can trigger memories in a person's mind about a pet he once owned or a place he once lived – memories that make him feel good all over. Recently I learned that veterinary schools all over the world are doing research on ways animals can improve the well-being of people in various therapeutic settings.

I always encourage people to read regular-print books as long as they can and then, later, when their eyesight is not as sharp, they can move to large-print books. When books of any kind are out of the question due to eyesight problems or difficulty in holding a book, "talking books" (books on tape) are the next best thing. Large-print books and books on tape are supplied free-of-charge by the Library of Congress through state and regional libraries to visually-impaired people and to people who are unable to hold a book.

Mrs. Hilda Koenig sometimes lets me help in the library when she updates the records. Keeping all the records is a big job for one person, or even two, so I am always happy to help.

Mrs. Koenig and I look at the library-user list with Mr. Richard Bottone, administrator of our retirement home.

One of the objectives of the Center for Animal Human Relationships (CENTAUR), an academic center for the study of the Human-Animal Interface, Virginia-Maryland Regional College of Veterinary Medicine, is to provide opportunities for motivational, educational, recreational, and/or therapeutic benefits to enhance quality of life... delivered in a variety of therapeutic environments in association with animals. CENTAUR will provide consultation groups interested in conducting projects in the human-animal bond...The Department of Psychiatry at MCV-VCU has already provided such a consultation in a contract with the Delta Society (a non-profit organization promoting mutually beneficial relationships with animals to improve people's health, independence and quality of life).

Excerpts from Charter
Center for Animal Human Relationships (CENTAUR)
VA-MD Regional College of Veterinary Medicine
Virginia Tech

In the Computer Room
Go online

People who keep in touch with the outside world have a decided edge over those who withdraw from interaction with others and retreat into their own minds. Accordingly, a therapy dog can do a better job of helping a person stay in touch with the world if the person cares about what's going on around him. The key seems to be to help people stay tuned in to happenings with people close by AND far away.

One way for a sick or non-mobile person to keep in touch with others is through the Internet. However, lots of our friends won't get close to a computer. I try to interest people in the Internet and encourage them to do e-mail. Sometimes, when they find out how much fun e-mail is, they go on to do more exciting things on the Web. Surfing the Web lets you walk around in a shopping mall, take in a concert, or shop in a big dog supply store without taking a step! (For resources that encourage Internet use by seniors, see p. 42).

I wish more of my friends could get the feel of the computer keyboard and what it can do. I am hoping to interest our community college in offering on-site, retirement home, beginning computer classes, because many of the residents are not physically able to go out in the community for classes held elsewhere. People who learn computer skills often gain a measure of confidence that affects their whole lives.

After Miss Sara Boggs logs on and checks her e-mail, she likes to play solitaire. When she offered to give me a few solitaire pointers, I took her up on it. She's an excellent teacher, and she seems to enjoy explaining solitaire to me.

Recent polls indicate that more than 13 million older Americans have discovered the home computer, including new Internet appliances and its ability to connect them to the Web and e-mail. In many, it has restored a vigor in life.

Eric Taub
"We're Logging On To The World"
Reprinted with Permission from
PARADE Copyright © 2000

If ever you're lacking some pep,
Computers can serve as your rep.
The Net is the way
To virtually stay
Afoot—without taking a step!

In the Hall
Dogs are not the only therapy pets

Mrs. Cora Chandler spends a lot of time in a wheelchair visiting with friends in one of the lounges or in the hall because she can't walk around anymore. We know it isn't fun relying on a wheelchair to get around, so we always try to give her a little lift. Because she can maneuver her chair by herself, she doesn't need us to take her for a walk. Just to stop, even for a few minutes, seems to brighten everything for her.

Mrs. Chandler and Winnie are talking about something important in the pictures below while I keep an eye on Petie who is in a birdcage just two leaps away. I must admit my focus has shifted from Mrs. Chandler to the bird. Nobody's perfect! That's one of the reasons Winnie and I like to make therapy rounds together. If one of us becomes distracted, the other carries on.

This energetic little Petie-bird brings a tiny bit of the outside world inside for people who spend most of their time indoors. That's the whole reason Petie-bird lives here. In the relatively new "Eden Alternative" which brings birds, animals and plants into healthcare facilities, one of the first steps is to introduce resident birds and fish. Birds and fish aren't nearly as much trouble to take care of as dogs, cats, rabbits and other animals would be. Just as Petie mesmerizes me, so people are drawn to his cheerful chirps as he flits around in his cage.

Petie and I compare notes
on our therapy activities.

Mrs. Chandler chats with Winnie
while I watch Petie.

Birds are small, inexpensive, social creatures that live long lives and are well suited to the nursing home environment. Birds provide the variety and spontaneity so often missing from nursing home life.

William H. Thomas, M.D.
Life Worth Living
VanderWyk & Burnham,
1996

In the Lounge
Plug in some music

The job of a therapy dog is to bring comfort to people who are sick or whose activities are severely restricted for one reason or another. If there is music in the air, people seem to feel better, and we do, too. The music can come from television or tapes, but a "live" person singing or playing is even better. Encouraging a resident we are visiting to sing or play pays off in several ways: 1) it gives the person a good feeling, 2) it makes a lively background mood for other people, and 3) it reminds Winnie and me to lighten up when doing therapy gets to us. It's a fact that a stroke victim who cannot speak can sometimes communicate through music. And it seems that people often comprehend better what Winnie and I are thinking when we are all listening to music.

I'd listen to good music all the time if I could. And Winnie would, too, but her taste is slightly different from mine. She wants country for daytime listening and classical at night. I'll take classical stuff most of the time along with a little jazz. If you've visited my website, you know that I'm big on music. On the opening page, I play "Heart and Soul" on the special Tom Hanks-like keyboard that my webmaster made for me.

Even though Mrs. Mary Sprague no longer teaches piano or plays the organ in her church, she can still play a million tunes on the piano. The halls ring with tunes of yesteryears when she stops at the piano outside the dining room and runs her hands over the keys. Because she seems to enjoy playing when there is an audience, we encourage her by sitting still and listening as long as she will play.

I believe that we learn from our relationships with animals the same things we learn from the language of music–that is: how to have loving spiritual and emotional relationships with ourselves.

Peter Dundon
Music Teacher
Unpublished Manuscript

Mrs. Sprague plays one of my favorite songs,
"Heart and Soul," for her grandson.

In the Conference Room
Take advantage of group activities

Most of our therapy work is done with one person at a time. However, we occasionally participate in a group activity if we are behind in our scheduled appointments. During a bingo game, for example, or prior to a Current Events session when residents are gathering, we can make contacts with several people at one time.

Current Events sessions are conducted weekly by knowledgeable leaders in the community. In the photo below, Winnie seems to be listening closely from Mrs. Josephine Custis's lap, but if the truth be known, Winnie is actually beginning to snuggle down for a nap. In five minutes, she was snoring away. I stayed focused on the speaker, however, for the entire session from Mrs. Virgelia Mapp's lap. During the whole session, Mrs. Mapp patted my head and rubbed my back which probably felt almost as good to her as it did to me. We've known Mrs. Mapp and Mrs. Custis for a long time; in fact, Mrs. Custis's college-age grandson, John, is one of our very best friends.

Mrs. Custis and Mrs. Mapp listen to the Current Events facilitator while giving us quality time.

Animals selected for AAA/AAT should be alert, bright, happy and healthy, playful without being too rowdy. They may be frisky without being overbearing. Dogs which appear withdrawn or submissive...should be avoided. They should be even-tempered, good-natured, and willing to withstand travel and environmental stress. They must not bite, snap, or snarl. They should have a distinct personality. Dogs must be easily controllable in a new environment and walk on a leash if necessary.

**Phil Arkow
Pet Therapy
Arkow, 8ᵗʰ Edition, 1998**

In the Workshop
Encourage activity

We're told it is really important for people to stay active in their retirement years. Mr. Fred Rux is one of our friends who is always busy working on a project. When he is not in his room, we look in the work-shop, where we can almost always find him.   One of his hobbies is can-ing chairs for people, but he does other handyman repair jobs, too. It's good that people can carry over skills and interests from their younger lives. That must mean that dogs can, too, which reminds me to think about developing another hobby. Chasing a tennis ball may not be so easy in the coming years.

Being low-to-the-ground dogs like us has advantages, but it works against us when we are trying to watch something at tabletop level. When Mr. Rux works on a chair, we can watch easily because he places the chair on a little platform that is just our height. He always talks about what he is doing while he works, probably the way he used to explain something to his sons when they were growing up. Mr. Rux doesn't see his sons often, now, because they live far away. Knowing he must get lonely for them, we like to cheer him up. In fact, we love to visit with him, encouraging him to keep up his handyman work and complimenting him on his good caning jobs.

**We like to talk shop with
Mr. Rux while he works on a chair**

Animal-assisted therapy is a new field with ancient roots. The connection between spiritual healing and animals goes back to the days of hunter-gather-ers. The Mayans believed that each per-son is assigned a "soul animal" as a guide through life. In the 19th century, Florence Nightingale recommended small pets for the chronically ill. Only in the 20th century did the medical pro-fession focus on animals, though more as a sanitation risk than a source of sol-ace.

In the last 20 years, after a 1980 study indicating that pet owners live longer than other people, research on the therapeutic benefits of animals has been on the rise.

**Julie V. Iovine
"Petropolis; The Healing Ways of Dr. Dog"
New York Times, October 28, 2001. ST-8**

But Not in the Dining Room
Respect rules

The dining room is off bounds to dogs. I guess that's okay. We have to respect rules because they were made for good reasons. However, it isn't always easy to understand why some rules were made, especially when we walk by the dining room at mealtime. When the aromas emanating from the dining room are particularly enticing, we try to point our noses dead ahead and keep walking straight! It helps if we have had a snack at home shortly before we make therapy rounds.

When I think about it, I realize that people probably don't need us as much in the dining room when they are seated at small tables eating with friends and talking with one another. Besides, most of them wouldn't have a hand free for petting a dog. Still, a whiff of hearty beef stew or just-out-of-the-pan crab cakes almost tears us up if we're hungry. Imagine the fun we'd have if we could throw fat calories to the wind, check in at twenty tables and get treats from fifty or sixty people at one time.

Therapy dogs may not go in the dining room for any reason.

Depending on the configuration of the institution, programs may be conducted in day rooms, central hallways, individual rooms, external courtyards, or other appropriate sites. Avoid dining and food service areas. Animal activities must not conflict with other programs. Waste removal, traffic flow, weather and patients' degree of ambulation must all be considered.

Phil Arkow
Pet Therapy
Arkow, 8th Edition, 1998

I AM A
THERAPY
DOG

Aboard An Electric Car
Adapt to circumstances

Ever since we've realized we could bring happiness to an elderly person without doing anything but being there, we have visited more often. As our friends become less mobile, they seem to need us more.

Now and then, to distract a person's thoughts from his pain or to raise his spirits if they are really low, Winnie and I clown around a little. In a small area, we can do a hilarious "catch-me-if-you-can" game, but we don't resort to horseplay often because it could get a person too worked up. Usually we stay relatively quiet. If the person is sick or lonely or confused, the little bit of happiness we offer can sometimes amount to more than we imagined. By the time our visit comes to an end, the person who had a sad, expressionless face when we arrived will have changed the sad expression to a happy face.

Our friend who has the coolest little electric car you've ever seen is Mr. Lance Eller. It is sort of like a small golf cart. Winnie has never gotten up the nerve to ride in it, but I climb up every time Mr. Eller invites me to take a ride with him. He is an excellent driver—I'd go anywhere with him. When we are driving around, he talks to me as if I were a real person. I dearly love to zoom up and down the long halls with him. "Zooming" isn't exactly the right word, but I pretend it is. I can see a lot more when I'm sitting up high in Mr. Eller's lap than from my usual vantage point.

As the first animal domesticated, the dog was not only man's earliest friend, but also his first therapist.

Odean Cusack and Elaine Smith
Pets and the Elderly
Haworth Press, 1984

When Mr. Eller and I are driving along,
both of us keep our eyes on the road

Indoors and Outdoors
Accompany a friend

One of our favorite therapy activities is to walk along with a person who is in a wheelchair. It makes Winnie and me feel important, and our friend enjoys our escort service. Sometimes we go outside, but if the weather is bad, we walk around inside. Almost any time is okay to do an inside walk. Residents love to take a spin through the halls because they are almost certain to run (not literally) into some friends they may not have seen for a time.

To venture outside, the weather has to be exactly right because most elderly people aren't accustomed to going in and out as many times a day as we are. If it is too hot or too cold or if the wind is blowing, we stay inside.

In the picture below, Miss Shari Rector helps us take Mrs. Mildred Peterson outside for a walk on a nice Indian summer day. As we keep in step with the turn of the wheels, Mrs. Peterson holds our leashes and talks to us. She is proof that even if you are in a wheelchair, you can have fun taking a couple of dogs for a walk.

IX. GIVE YOUR DOG A PURPOSE. Your dog needs to exercise his brain as much as he needs to exercise his body. Education, communication, exercise, play, and yes, even work can all stimulate your dog's mind and keep him happy.

Ross Becker
"The 10 Commandments of Dog Ownership"
Good Dog Magazine, July/August 1999

A walk outside feels good to everybody when the weather is good.

CHAPTER V

I'm Not a Spring Chicken Any Longer

It's not that nursing homes are going to the dogs: quite the opposite. The dogs are going to nursing homes–and every indication is that the homes' residents love it....Happiness really is a warm puppy.

Bill Lewis
"Pups Worth Weight in Therapeutic Gold to Home's Residents"

Pet therapy – aka pet visitation – involves taking your pet to visit people in need. Not only does this brighten the day of nursing home clientele, hospital patients and others, but it also provides real therapeutic benefits. Some people speak to the animals when they will no longer speak to people. Some people who resist more traditional physical therapy will happily grab a brush and comb a dog. It is delightful, challenging work for truly friendly people and dogs.

Brian Kilcommons and
Sarah Wilson
Paws to Consider
Warner Books, 1999

Graying around the Muzzle

Now that I have some age on me (Winnie keeps telling me I'm getting gray), I am much more comfortable with older people than when I was younger. It seems that age has given me a slant on life that helps me see things in a different light. I know, now, that fast is not always the best speed–walking instead of running is much more dignified and if you move along slowly, you see more on the way. It may be that a dog's therapy work cannot crest until some gray creeps in his muzzle. I'm sure I have a better idea of what it's like to be a senior citizen, now that I am getting to be one.

Often, I can tune in to the problems of my people friends better because I have experienced some of their plights. For example, arthritis slows me down when the weather is damp. Sometimes when I get up from a nap, stiff joints bother me if I try to start playing ball right away. But if I take time to do some stretching exercises, my legs don't feel jammed up and I can run more easily. Arthritis doesn't interfere with lots of other things like birdwatching and basking in the sun, so I say to myself, "Mick, you can't play ball all the time, anyhow. Just find something else to do for a while."

Without asking anything in return, Winnie and I try to help keep our elderly friends from feeling lonely by reminding them how it felt to have fun and feel like playing. Whereas a human who visits a sick or lonely person often takes flowers to brighten his day, we just take ourselves—and possibly two or three gentle love licks. From our point of view, love licks are better than pick-me-up bouquets, and they are always on tap. Love licks are free, too, and so are we.

The pleasure of animal companionship and the enjoyment of children, music, art, movement and touch are increasingly the focus of professional therapists and their treatment plans. Loneliness, helplessness and boredom are impervious to the silver bullets of modern medicine.

William H. Thomas, M.D.
Life Worth Living
VanderWyk and Burnham,
1996

I'm mentioning age for a reason,
The fact that I, too, am well seasoned
Enables me more–
To sense what before–
Might never have come to me easy!

Being Good Listeners Even When Seniors Harp on Their Health

Sometimes people don't understand when senior citizens go on and on about the health problems they are experiencing. When I was young, I always tried to listen attentively when older friends discussed their health, but sometimes it was hard for me to be interested. Now that I know how important health is to you whether you are a dog or a human, I'm a more patient listener.

Dr. Cameron reassures me after surgery.

I've got some medical stuff going on myself, but that doesn't mean I suddenly have to give up on life. Admittedly it was a blow when I heard my veterinarian, Dr. Paula Cameron, say, "Mickey, you've got cancer." It knocked the wind out of my sails. But lucky for me, Dr. Cameron scheduled surgery the very next day. She was able to remove the whole thing by making a five-inch incision which isn't to be sneezed at when you're my size. The procedure set me back, of course, but it did some good things for me, too: it fired me up to join the Great Cancer Chase and it helped me understand how special every day of life is. I've resolved to make the most of each day that comes along.

Last year, because I was recuperating from surgery, I couldn't join a Cancer Relay-for-Life race team until late in the season. But by putting a picture story about the Cancer Relay on my website, and by badgering my friends to contribute, I was able to help raise a nice piece of money for cancer research. This year, I have a feeling our dog team composed of twenty dogs and ten dog lovers with Dr. Cameron as our leader, will be able to raise much more money to help fight cancer.

As this book goes to press, my routine senior citizen checkup has just revealed two potential trouble spots–one, my heart and the other, my back legs. Dr. William Brewer has come into my life as my heart specialist, and Dr. Richard Seuss, orthopedic surgeon, is deciding what to do about my other problem. Meanwhile, I am filling my days with watching birds and squirrels, patrolling the front door, teasing Winnie and being a therapy dog. Actually, therapy dogging may be as much pleasure for me as it is for the people I visit.

Relay for Life

Is a Dog Qualified to Write a Book?

There are people who scoff at the idea that a dog knows how to write. I could whip out a long list of reasons proving a dog's ability to write, whether at a computer, with pen in paw, or by dictating the words to a secretary. However, knowing that my argument would be more convincing if it were offered by someone else, I defer to Diomed, a talented author of more than a century ago who was more adept with words than I shall ever hope to be.

Diomed was a famous hunting dog who wrote an intriguing account of his travels and life experiences in his book, <u>Diomed, the Life Travels and Observations of a Dog.</u> In the book, Diomed addresses readers of any century who would question a dog's ability to write. Had Diomed lived in this day and time, I'm sure he would have had his paws on a computer keyboard instead of being assisted by a stenographer.

You cannot deny that the brain of a dog possesses marvelous faculties of reason and memory. We love association with you, oftentimes better even than with our own kind. We seek companionship with you, more than creatures of any other race. And you, in your turn, oftentimes return this compliment. As for our hearts, you turn from mankind for a figure of speech to express loyalty and unselfishness of the highest type, and find the simile among us in the declaration that some human being is as "faithful as a dog." So, away, henceforth, if you please, with this talk about my incapacity to know, or think, or write these things, for I do know, have thought and felt, and can express them...And lastly, although an old fogey in years, my heart is young and my ideas are progressive; to the end I shall avail myself of all the modern aids to labor, among them the stenographer.

Diomed, The Life Travels and Observations of a Dog
John Sergeant Wise
Macmillan, 1899

Canine Applaws

Most of the quotations cited on previous pages have been words spoken or written by people. Because canine readers might enjoy knowing how dogs look at therapy work, it seems reasonable to include the thoughts of several canines at some point. My friends, *Jordan* (Bailey) and *Brooke* (Hayes) are veteran therapy dogs. *Bernie* (Randall) and *Dylan* (Robinson) hope to become licensed therapy dogs soon.

A great learning manual for new therapy pups. There's nothing like paws-on experience to pass on to others. Great insights on seniors for our humans, too.

Lion's Watch Nandua Jordan (Jordan), CGC, Pets on Wheels
(Golden Retriever)

Therapy is something I'd like to do. My show days are over. My breeding days are over – I had ten children, three of whom are champions. But I'm not retired from life. In fact, I'm full of it. Your book has motivated me to try something new!

CH Anchor's Tarbay's Burning Star (Bernie)
(Boston Terrier)

A MUST read for any dog interested in therapy work.

U-C.D. Sky Acres Ashe Brooke, (Brooke), C.D., C.G.C., T.D.I., V.C.C.X. B.P.D.K., Delta Pet Partner
National Therapy Dog of the Year 1999
(Belgian Tervuren)

I was really glad when my first birthday came along and I was declared old enough to become a real therapy dog because I've enjoyed being an everyday therapy dog at home for some time. Soon, I'll have some dog-degree letters beside my name, too!

Justin Analyst from Winsom (Dylan)
(Norwich Terrier)

**Dylan began doing therapy at home with his mom,
Mrs. Betty Robinson, before he was old enough to meet the
requirements for therapy dog certification.**

Afterbark

All in all, I love being a therapy dog even though it's strenuous work for Winnie and me to be on our toes every minute we are making our rounds. We can give therapy our full attention for about an hour or hour-and-a-half max. After that, we get on edge if we can't call it a day. To decompress, we simply cut up and act silly for a little while or race around or play ball. This always helps us settle down enough to level out and look forward to whatever comes up next.

Mickey

Mickey has done it again! He and his "secretary" have produced a comprehensive, informative, and easy to read book which will introduce the reader to Mickey and his best friend Winnie's experiences as therapy dogs.

As a former owner of a therapy dog, I can attest that therapy pets bring great joy to the residents of nursing homes and to other individuals who, for various reasons, are not able to leave their residences. These people look forward with great anticipation to the arrival of their four-legged friends, who challenge them to think of the happy experiences they enjoyed with their own pets. The smiles these therapy animals bring to the faces of folks who are not able to get out and about are priceless. Seeing the pleasure they receive from petting and holding these animals makes it all worthwhile.

Betty Robinson
Unpublished Manuscript

Organizations, Websites, Addresses, Links

Healthcare & "of Senior Citizen Interest" Organizations

AARP Health and Welfare
www.aarp.org/indexes/health.html

AARP information on nursing home quality
www.aarp.org/confacts/health/choosingnh.html

AARP National Headquarters
1909 K St., NW, Washington, DC 20049
www.aarp.org/indexes/health.html#caregiving

First Gov for Seniors (formerly Access America for Seniors)
www.seniors.gov

Administration on Aging
National Aging Information Center
330 Independence Ave, SW, Washington, DC 20201
202-619-0724 (other phone numbers listed on website for various kinds of info)
www.aoa.gov

Alliance for Retired Americans
www.retiredamericans.org

American Association of Homes and Services for the Aging - AAHSA
www.aahsa.org/public/consumer.htm
202-783-2242

American Geriatrics Society
The Empire State Building
350 Fifth Ave., Suite 801, New York, NY 10118
212-308-1414
www.americangeriatrics.org

American Health Care Association (AHCA)
1201 L Street, N.W., Washington, DC 20005
202-842-4444
www.ahca.org

Career Nurse Assistants
National Network of Career Nursing Assistants
3577 Easton Rd, Norton, Ohio 44203
www.cna-network.org

Center for Medicare Advocacy
P. O. Box 350, Willimantic, CT 06226
860-456-7790; 1-800-262-4414 in CT; 202-216-0028 in Washington, DC
www.medicareadvocacy.org

Center for Health Systems Research and Analysis (CHSRA)
University of Wisconsin - Madison
11th Floor, WARF Bldg.
610 Walnut St., Madison, WI 53705-2397
608-263-5722
www.chsra.wisc.edu

Center for Quality Health Care Services and Consumer Protection, Va. Dept. of Health
3600 W. Broad St., Section 216, Richmond, VA 23230
804-367-2102
www.vdh.state.va.us

The Rehabilitation Accreditation Commission (CARF)
4891 E. Grant Rd., Tucson, AZ 87512
520-325-1044
www.carf.org

Concerned Relatives of Nursing Home Patients
P. O. Box 18820, Cleveland Heights, OH 44118
216-321-0403

Consumer Consortium On Assisted Living (CCAL)
P. O. Box 3375, Arlington, VA 22203
1-703-533-8121
www.ccal.org

Continuing Care Accreditation Commission (CCAC)
202-783-2242
www.ccaconline.org/links.htm (great links page)

Continuing Care Retirement Communities (CCRC)
www.ccaconline.org/aflist.htm

Eldercare Locator
800-677-1116
www.aoa.dhhs.gov/elderpage/locator.html

Eden Alternative, Philosophy of Long-Term Care
www.edenalt.com

ElderWeb
www.elderweb.com

Gerontological Society of America
1030 15th St., NW, Suite 250, Washington, DC 20005
202-842-1275
www.geron.org

Health Hippo
http://hippo.findlaw.com

Hermitage, Eastern Shore
23610 North St., Onancock, VA 23417
757-787-4343
www.hermitage-hes.com

Joint Commission on Accreditation of Healthcare Organizations - JCAHO
One Renaissance Blvd., Oakbrook Terrace, IL 60181
630-792-5000
www.jcaho.org/trkgen_frm.html (for general public section)

Medicare information about nursing home issues and state regulators
www.medicare.gov/Nursing/Overview.asp

National Association of Professional Geriatric Care Managers
1604 N. Country Club Rd., Tucson, AZ 85715
521-881-8808
www.caremanager.org

National Citizens Coalition for Nursing Home Reform
1424 16th St. NW, Suite 202, Washington, DC 20036
202-332-2275, FAX-202-332-2949
www.nccnhr.org (from this site, you can go easily to state-by-state ombudsmen)

National Council on the Aging
409 Third St. SW, Washington, D.C. 20024
202-479-1200
www.ncoa.org

National Institute on Aging
P. O. Box 8057, Gaithersburg, MD 20898
800-222-2225,   301-496-1752
www.nih.gov/nia

Nursing Home Compare
www.medicare.gov/nhcompare/home.asp

Pioneers
Rose Marie Fagan, Exec. Director
Pioneer Network
1900 S. Clinton Ave, P. O. Box 18648
Rochester, NY 14618
916-244-8400, ext. 115
www.pioneernetwork.net

Radio Show - A Touch of Grey
www.atouchofgrey.com

Senior Journal
The Episcopal Society of Ministry on Aging
www.seniorjournal.com

Senior Health Center
www.seniorhealth.about.com/health/seniorhealth
(connects to 700 sites - good info)

Health Central - Senior Health
www.healthcentral.com/centers/onecenter.cfm?center=seniorhealth

United Methodist Association of Health & Welfare
Ministries (UMA)
www.umassociation.org

United Seniors Health Cooperative
1331 H St, NW, Suite 500, Washington, DC 20005
202-393-6222
www.unitedseniorshealth.org

Virginia Assoc. of Nonprofit Homes for the Aging (VANHA)
4201 Dominion Blvd., Suite 100, Glen Allen, VA 23060
804-965-5500
FAX 804-965-9089
www.vanha.org

Virginia Health Care Association
804-353-9101

Virginia United Methodist Homes, Inc. (VUMH)
7113 Three Chopt Rd., Suite 300
Richmond, VA 23226-3643
804-673-1031

Senior Legal Resources

Senior Law
www.seniorlaw.com

ElderLaw Answers
www.elderlawanswers.com
(view State specific information on website)

Commission on Legal Problems of the Elderly
American Bar Association
1800 M St., NW, South Lobby, Washington DC 20036
202-662-8690
www.abanet.org/elderly (slow to load but worth it)

AARP Legal Services Network
601 E St., NW, Washington, DC 20049
800-424-3410
www.aarp.org/lsn

National Academy of Elder Law Attorneys
1604 North Country Club Rd, Tucson, AZ 85715
520-881-4005
www.naela.com
.
National Senior Citizens Law Center (NSCLC)
1101 14th St. NW, Suite 400, Washington, DC 20005
www.nsclc.org

Senior Citizen Activities in General

Horizons - American Express
www.americanexpress.com/senior

Organizations promoting Internet Use by Senior Citizens

AARP - Computers & Technology
601 E. St., NW, Washington, DC 20049
1-800-424-3410
www.aarp.org/comptech

Learn The Net
www.learnthenet.com

Senior Net
121 Second St., 7th Floor, San Francisco, CA 94105
415-495-4990
www.seniornet.com

Virginia's Health & Aging Resource
www.seniornavigator.com

Online Community for Seniors
www.senior.com

TechRiders
Alexandria, VA
knep@pilotonline.com

National & Regional Pet Therapy Associations

Animal Friends - Pet Therapy Program (super links)
http://trfn.clpgh.org/animalfriends/pet-therapy.html

Anthrozoology Institute
University of Southampton, England
www.soton.ac.uk/~azi/azi.htm

ASPCA
www.aspca.org

Canine Companions for Independence
National Headquarters
2965 Dutton Ave, P. O. Box 446
Santa Rosa, CA 95402
707-577-1700
www.caninecompanions.org

Censhare- University of Minnesota
www.censhare.umn.edu

Delta Society
580 Naches Avenue SW, Suite 101, Renton, WA 98055-2297
425-226-7357
www.deltasociety.org
http://petsforum.com/deltasociety/default.html

Dr. Hunt's Dog Page
www.cofc.edu/~huntc/service.html

Fidos for Freedom
P. O. Box 5508, Laurel, MD 20726
410-880-4178
www.fidosforfreedom.org

Fur, Fins & Feathers M.D.
www.furfinsfeathers.com

Foundation for Pet Provided Therapy
3809 Plaza Drive, #107-309, Oceanside, CA 92056
619-630-4824
www.fppt.org

Friendship Foundation
San Francisco, California
www.dog-play.com/friendship.html

Furry Friends - Pet Assisted Therapy Services
San Jose, California
www.furryfriends.org

Good Dog Foundation
607 6th Street
Brooklyn, NY 11215
www.thegooddogfoundation.org

Human Animal Bond Association of Canada
1 Stafford Rd., Ste. 182, Nepean, Ont.
Canada K2H 1B9
613-592-3676
www.home.istar.ca/~habac

Intermountain Therapy Animals
P.O. Box 17201, Salt Lake City UT 84117
801-485-1121 fax - 801-485-1131
www.therapyanimals.org

The Latham Foundation
Latham Plaza Bldg.
1826 Clement Ave., Alameda, CA 95401
510-521-0920 fax- 510-521-9861
www.latham.org

Love on a Leash
3809 Plaza Dr., #1070309, Oceanside, CA 92056
619-630-4824
www.loveonaleash.org

National Capitol Therapy Dogs, Inc.
www.nctdinc.org

Northeast Rehab Hospital Facilitated Program
www.rehabnet.com/aft/index.html
Paws for Health
Medical College of Virginia
http://views.vcu.edu/mcv/paws

Pawsitive Interaction
www.pawsitiveinteraction.org

People-Pet Partnership
School of Veterinary Medicine
Washington State University
www.vetmed.wsu.edu/depts-pppp/index.htm

Pet Therapy Society of Northern Alberta
330, 9768 170th St., Edmonton, AB
Canada T5T 5L4
780-413-4682
www.shopalberta.com/paws

Pets & People: Companions in Therapy & Service(AL)
http://www.petsandpeople.org/index.htm

Pets on Wheels of Prince George's County
www.pgpetsonwheels.org

Richards Therapy Dog Program
www.doglogic.com/therapy.htm

San Francisco SPCA
San Francisco, California
www.sfspca.org/aat.html

Share Program
Marin Humane Society, Marin, California
www.marinhumanesociety.org

Southwest Canine Corps of Volunteers
Albuquerque, NM
www.nmia.com/~dmiller

St. John's Ambulance Therapy Dog Program
532 Garside Dr., Peterborough, ON Canada K9H 7C7
705-755-1003

Superdog Animal Assisted Therapy
www.superdog.com/therapy.htm

Therapet Animal Assisted Therapy Foundation
P. O. Box 1696, Whitehouse, TX 75791-1696
www.therapet.com

Therapy Animals
International Delta Society. Utah
www.therapyanimals.org

Therapy Dogs, Inc.
P. O. Box 5868, Cheyenne, WY 82003
877-843-7364
www.therapydogs.com

Therapy Dogs of Vermont
www.therapydogs.org

Therapy Dogs International, Inc.
88 Bartley Road, Flanders, NJ 07836
975-252-9800
www.tdi-dog.org

Utah Animal-Assisted Therapy Association
www.aros.net/~uaata

Other Dog Sites

American Chesapeake Club
P.O. Box 58082, Salt Lake City, UT 84158
www.amchessieclub.org/TherapyDog.html

Animal Facilitated Therapy
Northeast Rehab Health Network
70 Butler St., Salem, NH 03079
www.northeastrehab.com/Programs/aft.htm

Breed Apart Greyhound Magazine
www.abap.org/Therapy2.htm

Dogs As Medicine
www.dog-play.com/dogpill.html

DogLogic
3020 Brown Ave., #10, Manchester, N.H. 03103
603-668-8157
www.doglogic.com

Dog Owners Guide - New Horizons for Therapy Dogs
www.canismajor.com/dog/hmless.html

Dog-Play
www.dog-play.com (super links)

Therapy Dog References
www.rahul.net/hredlus/therapy.html

Professional Dog Health Organizations
& Educational Organizations

AKC Canine Good Citizen Dept.
919-852-3875
www.akc.org/love/cgc/index.cfm

American Animal Hospital Association
P. O. Box 159899, Denver, CO 80215-0899
303-986-2800
www.aahhanet.org

American Board of Veterinary Practitioners
530 Church St., Suite 7900, Nashville, TN 37219
www.abvp.com

American Veterinary Medical Association (AVMA)
1931 N. Meacham Rd., Suite 100
Schaumburg, IL 60173
847-925-8070, FAX 847-925-1329
www.avma.org

American Veterinary Medical Foundation (AVMF)
1931 N. Meacham Rd., Suite 100
Schaumburg, IL 60173
800-248-2852, ext. 600
www.avmf.org

Association of American Veterinary Medical Colleges (AAVMC)
1101 Vermont Ave. NW, Suite 710
Washington, DC 20005
202-371-9195
www.aavmc.org

Association of Small Animal Practitioners
178 Peachtree Street, #299, Atlanta, GA 30303
800-PRO-0748

Canadian Veterinary Medical Association
339 Booth Street, Ottawa, Ontario
Canada K1R 7K1
613-236-1162
www.cvma-acmv.org

Center for the Human-Animal Bond
Purdue University School of Veterinary Medicine
www.vet.purdue/edu/chab/person.htm

Center for the Interaction of Animals and Society
School of Veterinary Medicine, University of Pennsylvania
www.vet.upenn.edu/cias

FDA Center for Veterinary Medicine
www.fda.gov/cvm

International Corres. School of Veterinary Assistants
925 Oak Street, Scranton, PA 18515
800-595-5505, ext. 1895
www.icslearn.com/ics/courses.htm

North American Veterinary Technician Association
P. O. Box 224, Battle Ground, IN 47920
317-742-2216
www.avma.org/navta/default.htm

Student American Veterinary Medical Asso. (SAVMA)
www.avma.org/savma/default.htm

Virginia Academy of Small Animal Medicine
P. O. Box 505, Maury, NC 28554

Virginia Federation of Dog Clubs and Breeds
moorgreen@aol.com

Virginia Veterinary Medical Association
4001 Springfield Rd., Glen Allen, VA 23060
800-VESVVMA

Washington University
Division of Comparative Medicine
Ken Boschert, D.V.M.
Box 8061, 660 Euclid Ave
St. Louis, Missouri 63110
http://netvet.wustl.edu

Dog Magazines and Newsletters

AKC Gazette - American Kennel Club
51 Madison Avenue, New York, NY 10010
-or-
580 Centerview Dr., Raleigh, NC 27606-3390
www.akc.org/pubs/index.cfm

Boston Terrier Club of America
www.bostonterrierclubofamerica.org

Canine Chronicle
4422 Orange Grove Dr., Houston, TX 77039

Dog & Kennel Magazine
7-L Dundas Circle, Greensboro, NC 27407
336-292-4047
www.dogandkennel.com

Dog Fancy Magazine
3 Burroughs, Irvine, CA 92618
-or-
P. O. Box 52364, Boulder, CO 80322-3264
800-365-4421
www.dogfancy.com

Dog Watch
Cornell University College of Veterinary Medicine Newsletter
www.vet.cornell.edu/publicresources/dog.htm

DOGWORLD Magazine
29 N. Wacker Drive, Chicago, IL 60606
800-365-4421
www.dogworldmag.com

Dogs in Canada
Canadian Kennel Club
89 Skyway Avenue, Suite 200
Etobicoke, Ontario M9W 6R4, Canada
416-798-9778
www.dogs-in-canada.com

Fetching the Paper
Pawprince Press
815 Clark Rd., Maldemount, WA 60606

Good Dog! Magazine   (great articles)
P. O. Box 10069, Austin, TX 78766
www.gooddogmagazine.com

North American Dog
Dogs International
P. O. Box 2270, Alpine, OH 91903
800-364-3283

Your Dog, A Magazine for Caring Dog Owners
Tufts University School of Veterinary Medicine
200 Westboro Road, North Grafton, MA 01536
www.tufts.edu/vet/publications/yourdog/index.html

College and University based Internet Sites related to Dogs

(information below obtained from April 2001 issue of Dog Watch, Reliable Dog Sites, Cornell University College of Veterinary Medicine Newsletter)

University of Illinois College of Veterinary Medicine's Pet Column
www.cvm.uiuc.edu/ceps/petcolumns

University of Wisconsin (Dr. Mark Plonsky, psychologist and dog trainer)
www.uwsp.edu/psych/dog/lib-prob.htm

Virginia Tech
Virginia Maryland Regional College of Veterinary Medicine Center for Animal Human Relationships (CENTAUR)
www.vetmed.vt.edu/centaur

Encyclopedia of Canine Veterinary Medical Information (Michael Richards, DVM)
www.vetinfo.com/dencyclopedia/deindex.html

Columbia Animal Hospital, Columbia, Maryland
www.cah.com/library

Veterinary Medical Encyclopedia
www.vetcentric.com/reference/encyc.cfm

links to a variety of dog-related sites including non-profit organizations and newsgroups
www.dogfriendly.com/articles

National Kennel Clubs

American Kennel Club
5580 Centerview Drive, Raleigh, NC 27606-3390
919-233-9767
www.akc.org

American Rare Breed Association
9921 Frank Tippett Rd, Cheltenham, MD 20623
301-868-5718
www.arba.org

Canadian Kennel Club
Commerce Park
89 Skyway Avenue, Suite 100
Etobicoke, Ontario M9W 6R4
414-675-5511
www.ckc.ca

United Kennel Club, Inc.
100 E. Kilgore Road, Kalamazoo, Michigan 49002-5584
616-343-9020
www.ukcdogs.com

United States Kennel Club
325 West 29th Street, Hialeah, FL 33012
305-885-3008
www.uskennelclub.qpg.com

Other Dog related organizations

American Society for the Prevention of Cruelty to Animals (ASPCA)
441 East 92nd Street, NY, NY 10028
212-876-7700
www.aspca.org

Association of Pet Dog Trainers
P. O. Box 385, Davis, CA 95617
800-PET-DOGS
www.apdt.com

Dog Writers Association of America (DWAA)
www.dwaa.org

National Association of Dog Obedience Instructors
Private Mail Box 369
729 Gravevine Highway, Suite 369, Hurst, TX 76054-2085
www.nadoi.org

DogWriters Association

DWAA (see above)

Bibliography

<u>Books</u>
Abdill, Margaret N. and Juppe, Denise. Pets in Therapy. Idyll Arbor, Inc. , 1997.
Arkow, Phil. Pet Therapy: A Study and Resource Guide for the Use of Companion Animals in Selected Therapies, March 1998.
Becker, Marty, DVM. The Healing Power of Pets. Hyperion, 2002.
Bergin, Bonnie. Understanding "Dog Mind." Little Brown and Co., 2000.
Burch, Mary R. Volunteering with Your Pet. Howell Book House, 1996.
Bush, Millie. Millie's Book as Dictated to Barbara Bush. Quill, NY, 1990.
Conant, Susan. The Barker Street Regulars. Bantam Books, 1999.
Cusack, Odean and Smith, Elaine. Pets and the Elderly, The Therapeutic Bond. Haworth Press, NY, NY, 1984.
Davis, Kathy Diamond. Therapy Dogs: Training Your Dog to Reach Others. Howell, NY, NY, 1992.
Davis, Tom. Why Dogs Do That. Willow Creek Press. Minocqua, Wisconsin, 1998.
DeVito, Carlo and Ammens, Amy. The Everything Dog Book. Adams Media Corporation, 1999.
Dibra, Bash. Dog Speak. Simon & Schuster, NY, 1999.
Esordi, Renee Lamm. You Have A Visitor. Blue Lamm Publishing, 2000.
Fields-Babineau, Miriam. The Aging Dog. T. F. H. Publications. NJ.
Fine, Aubrey, ed. Handbook on Animal-Assisted Therapy. Academic Press, 2000.
Fogle, Bruce. K-I-S-S, Guide to Living with a Dog. Dorling Kindersley, London, 2000.
Goodall, Jane. Dr. White. North-South Books, NY, NY, 1999.
Grenier, Roger. The Difficulty of Being a Dog. University of Chicago Press. Chicago, Illinois 2000.
Hart, Lynette. "Psychosocial Benefits of Animal Companionship" from Fine, Aubrey: Handbook on Animal-Assisted Therapy, cited above
Hodgson, Sarah. Complete Idiot's Guide to Choosing, Training and Raising a Dog, The. Alpha Books, 1996.
Kilcommons, Brian and Wilson, Sarah. Paws to Consider. Warner Books, 1999.
King, Julius. Dogs. Thomas Nelson & Sons, NY, 1927.
Labreche, Julianne. Best Friends: Therapy Dogs Helping Aphasic Adults. Primrose Court Publications, Ottawa, Ontario, 2001.
Lacey, Ann H. and Pratt, Barbara Wunder. Dr. Rickey, Wednesday's Promise. St. Vincent Press, 1997.
Lieberman, Trudy, ed. et al. Consumer Reports Complete Guide to Health Services for Seniors. Three Rivers Press, NY, 2000
Lingenfelter, Mike and Frei, David. The Angel by My Side. Hay House, Inc. Carlsbad, CA., 2002
Meade, Scottee. The Boston Terrier. Howell, 2000
Miller, Lucinda and Suthers-McCabe, Marie. 4-H PetPALS. Ohio State University Extension, 2002.
Morris, Virginia. How to Care for Aging Parents. Workman Publishing, 1996. Alpha Books, 2001.
Pavia, Audrey. Careers with Dogs. Barron's, NY, 1998.
Rantz, Marilyn, Popejoy, Lori, Zwygart-Stauffacher. The New Nursing Homes. Fairview Press, 2001.
Rhodes, Linda. Complete Idiot's Guide to Caring for Aging Parents, The. Alpha Books, Indianapolis, IN, 2001.
Root, Jacqueline. Organization and Management of a K-9 Therapy Group. Denlinger Publishers, 1990.
Ruckert, Janet, ed. The Four-Footed Therapist. Ten Speed Press, Berkeley, CA, 1987.
Rosen, Michael J., Ed., 21st Century Dog, A Visionary Compendium. Stewart, Tabori & Chang, NY, 2000.
Sanders, Clinton R. Understanding Dogs. Temple University Press, Philadelphia. 1999.
Schoen, Allen M. Kindred Spirits. Broadway Books, NY. 2001.
Taylor, David. The Family Dog. Barron's, NY. 2001.
Thomas, William H. Life Worth Living. VanderWyk and Burnham, Acton, MA, 1996.
Thornton, Kim and Guidry, Virginia. For the Love of Dogs. Publications International, Ltd., Lincolnwood, IL, 1997.
Volhard, Jack and Wendy. The Canine Good Citizen, Every Dog Can Be One. Howell, NY, NY, 1994.
Walton, Joel and Adamson, Eve. Labrador Retrievers for Dummies. IDG Books Worldwide, 2000.
Washington State University, College of Veterinary Medicine. How to Start a People-Pet Partnership Program. 1999.
Wise, John Sergeant. Diomed. Grosset & Dunlap, NY, 1899.
Wynn, William J., Judge. It's the Law! (Pets, Animals and The Law). Doral Publishing, Sun City, Arizona, 2002.

<u>Bulletins, Magazines, Newsletters, Newspaper Articles</u>
Arden, Darlene. "The Healing Bond." AKC Gazette, October 2000.
Barker, Sandra. "A Doggone Good Time." Portsmouth Currents, The Virginian-Pilot, Norfolk, VA, 1/7/01.
Becker, Ross. "The 10 Commandments of Dog Ownership." Good Dog Magazine, July/August 1999.
Cornell University College of Veterinary Medicine Newsletter, Dog Watch, selected issues, 1999, 2000.
Crary, David. "Internet touted as '90s e-lixir to pep up nursing home elderly." The Virginian-Pilot, Norfolk, VA, 11/22/99.
Gallagher, Cynthia. "The Dogtor Is In" Dog and Kennel, June 2001.
Iovine, Julie V.. "Petropolis," The Healing Ways of Dr. Dog., The New York Times, 10/28/01.
Palika, Liz "Can You and Your Dog Be a Therapy Team?" Dog Fancy, 8/97, pp. 84-86.
Rugg, Leslie Crane. "Canine Nature, The Spirit That Keeps Giving." Dog and Kennel, April 2002.
Roosevelt, Margot. "Canine Candy Stripers." Time, August 5, 2001.
Swinn, Brian. "Paws for Healing" Dog and Kennel, August 2001.
Taub, Eric. "We're Logging on to the World." Parade Magazine, 11/26/00.
Taylor, Roberta. "Sussex Co. LPN Program Pharmacology Worksheet." www.dog-play.com/dogpill.html.
Tennant, Diane. "Good Dogs, Good Deeds." The Virginian-Pilot, Norfolk. VA 12/2/00.
Therapy Dog International Newsletters, 1999, 2000.
Tufts University School of Veterinary Medicine Newsletter, Your Dog, selected issues, 1999, 2000.

Index

A portion of the proceeds from the sale of
LapDog Therapy
will benefit

Therapy Dogs International, Inc. (TDI)
Tel. 973-252-9800; Fax 973-252-7171; tdi@gti.net; www.tdi-dog.org

and

Hermitage on the Eastern Shore
A Continuing Care Retirement Community
Onancock, VA
757-787-4343, 888-437-8864
www.hermitage-hes.com

To order
LapDog Therapy
My Journey from Companion Dog to Therapy Dog

call

1-800-788-3196

or Write:

American Heritage Collection
9004 H Yellow Brick Road
Baltimore, Maryland 21237

This book is a treasure trove of simple poignant messages for all of us - canine and human. Mickey and Winnie teach us that they, like human therapists, can enrich others' lives by being authentic, gentle and well-mannered. Like their human counter-parts, they create a therapeutic environment by their presence and their special training. Mickey and Winnie serve as role models for their human friends. They teach us that our lives become enriched when we use our talents to be kind to others. They teach us that we all need to connect with other living creatures.

Peggy Swan
Professional Counselor

www.bostonsworld.com

Acknowledgements
by
Mickey

To thank to all the people who have helped with this book would be a Mastiff-sized task. Nevertheless, I would like to name some of them and hope the others will understand they are included. First of all, I owe at least 1000 licks to the residents and staff of the Hermitage on the Eastern Shore because they set the tone for the whole book. Without their warm welcome, I wouldn't have had a story to tell.

My thanks go to Therapy Dogs International for having its therapy dog framework, training guidelines, and certified evaluators in place. Because TDI was set up to license therapy dogs, Winnie and I have been able to function in this capacity - and to think of the possibility of writing about it.

In my wildest dreams, I hadn't imagined anything even remotely related to original watercolors for my book. The illustrations I envisioned were color photographs with some nice line drawings sprinkled in. All of that changed when Dr. Paula Cameron surprised me by painting eight wonderful Boston-y watercolors that give heart and soul to the book. Added to my appreciation of Dr. Cameron's remarkable talent as an artist, I owe much to her as a highly-skilled veterinarian who has cared for Winnie and me for most of our lives.

I wish to thank Dr. Marie Suthers-McCabe, director of CENTAUR, the Center for Animal-Human Relationships at the VA-MD School of Veterinary Medicine, who glimpsed potential in the book early on and encouraged me to get it finished. Dr. Suthers-McCabe's desire to teach 4-H groups how to use therapy dogs in healthcare/retirement facilities led to the Virginia Tech Foundation's interest in partnering with me to obtain funding from the Widgeon Foundation to publish and distribute the book. Thanks are also due to Dr. Frank Pearsall, development director for the Virginia Tech Veterinary School, who successfully shepherded the Widgeon grant through the approval process and who will administer it.

To my West Coast friend, Dr. Barbara Cox, I owe profound thanks for her idea of creating PowerPoint presentations to make the book more interactive. She and Dr. Suthers-McCabe, both of whom are PowerPoint experts, have combined forces to build custom presentations for veterinary and medical school students, dog-minded groups and civic clubs.

Mrs. Betty Robinson had known the joys of owning an active therapy dog some years ago. More recently, following a stroke, she was on the receiving end of a healthy dose of canine therapy in a rehabilitation center. Mrs. Robinson shares my passion to put therapy dog information into the hands of professional healthcare people and dog lovers alike. Through the Widgeon Foundation, she made it happen like magic! My heartfelt thanks go to Mrs. Robinson for launching LapDog Therapy in such a wonderful and far-reaching way.

Our relatives, neighbors and friends must have grown tired of hearing about my book over the past several years, but they were always good sports to let me ramble on about whatever I was working on at the time. It has been helpful to have friends, both people and dogs, who share our interests, and I send special licks and kisses to all of them.

Also I am indebted to:
- author Dave Frei, one of our nation's leading advocates of therapy dogging, who helped me not only with the text but also with telling others about the book;
- artist Julie Parker who created the Boston pen-and-ink sketches;
- novelist Lenore Poyer who improved the text considerably when she and her writing workshop students teamed up with me;
- computer guru Evan Clements who helped me understand my computer on many occasions and who enhanced many of the photographs;
- my special friends Renia Davis and Momma who rode many extra miles to help execute the book;
- the authors and publishers who permitted me to extract quotes from their books, magazine and newspaper articles;
- Sarah Nock who improved the manuscript immeasurably by applying good judgement and superb editing skills throughout the development of the book. I could never have finished it without her help; and
- Concept II Graphics and Printing, who, under Al Johnson's direction, transformed my work into a book that is both informative and professional. The attention to detail and creative ideas offered by Mr. Johnson and his production staff were unfaltering to the end. Winnie and Mom join me in thanking everyone at Concept II, including third generation Lexi, who at age 2 is already beginning to learn the printing business.

Lexi discusses printing details with me.